Modified Basic Ski

Correcting Word Reversals

by Penny Groves

Table of Contents

Introduction

It is not unusual for young learners to reverse letters and words—that is, to print them in a backward formation. The sooner children learn the correct direction, the sooner they will feel successful in all areas of study.

Teachers do not need a background in special education to use *Correcting Word Reversals*. Any teacher who observes a child making numerous letter or word reversals can strengthen the child's progress in producing the correct formations.

The initial set of exercises in *Correcting Word Reversals* focuses on being aware of the difference between "right" and "left." Without this foundation, the learning process will be more difficult. Next, pages with fine-motor activities require the child to use the left-to-right concept when working on the correct sequence of letters in a word or words in a sentence. Each exercise uses visual, auditory, and tactile components. The child touches an arrow and word and traces them from left to right. As the exercises progress, the child reads a short sight word. The teacher should read the sentence aloud while the child reads and tracks along to the right.

A more advanced stage of development requires a child to identify the position of letters in words without reversing the image of the letters. Exercises in this book will strengthen awareness of several easily reversed letters. More challenging exercises follow and focus on identifying the position of easily reversed letters in isolated words as well as reversed words in sentences.

Correcting Word Reversals can have a great impact on establishing the correct foundation to identify and to write letters and words as expected.

Published by LDA
an imprint of
Frank Schaffer Publications®

Author: Penny Groves
Editors: Debra Olson Pressnall, D'Arlyn Marks, Mary Hassinger
Cover Artists: Terri Moll and Peter Lochner
Interior Designer: Mark Conrad
Interior Artist: Janet Armbrust, based on drawings by Penny Groves
Photo Credits: ©EyeWire

Frank Schaffer Publications®

LDA is an imprint of Frank Schaffer Publications.

Send all inquiries to:
Frank Schaffer Publications
3195 Wilson Drive NW
Grand Rapids, Michigan 49534

Correcting Word Reversals

ISBN: 0-7424-0269-X

4 5 6 7 8 9 10 PAT 09 08 07

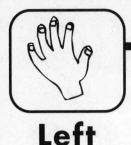

Left

Name: _____

Right

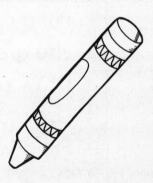

Directions:

1. Circle the toy by the boy's **right** foot.
2. Put an **X** on his **right** arm.
3. Color his **right** shoe red.
4. Use yellow to color his **right** sock.
5. Put a flower in his **right** hand.
6. Draw a bug on his **right** leg.

0-7424-0269-X *Correcting Word Reversals*

Left

Right

Directions:

1. Put an **X** under the girl's **left** foot.
2. Use green to color her **left** shoe.
3. Draw a circle around her **left** hand.
4. Use red to color her **left** sock.
5. Put a yellow bandage on her **left** leg.
6. Draw blue dots on the **left** side of her dress.

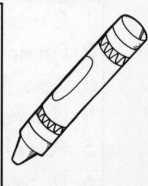

4 0-7424-0269-X *Correcting Word Reversals*

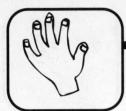

Left

Name:

Right

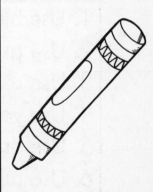

Directions:

1. Use red to color the clown's **right** shoe.
2. Use blue to color the clown's **left** hand.
3. Use green to color the clown's **left** sock.
4. Put an **X** on the clown's **left** leg.
5. Put a balloon in the clown's **right** hand.
6. Use yellow to color the clown's **right** sock.

0-7424-0269-X *Correcting Word Reversals*

Review of Left and Right

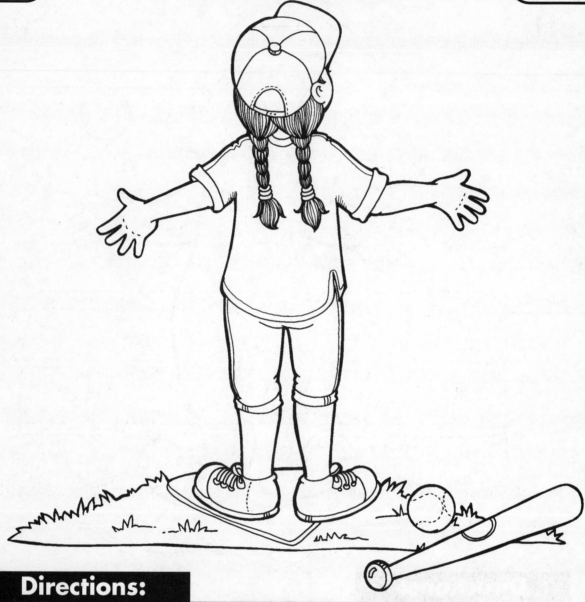

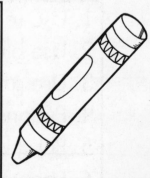

Directions:

1. Use blue to color the **right** sleeve.
2. Use green to color the **left** sleeve.
3. Use red to color **right** sock.
4. Use yellow to color the **left** sock.
5. Use orange to color the **right** shoe.
6. Use purple to color the **left** shoe.

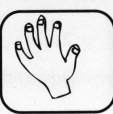

Review of Left and Right

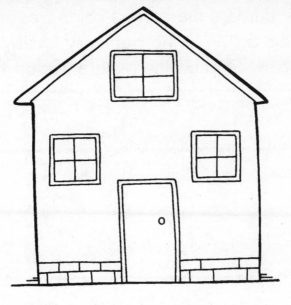

Directions:

1. Put an **X** to the **left** of the ball.
2. Put a • to the **right** of the wall.
3. Draw a flower to the **left** of the house.
4. Draw a bug to the **right** of the ball.
5. Draw a circle to the **left** of the wall.
6. Draw grass to the **right** of the house.

0-7424-0269-X *Correcting Word Reversals*

Name: _____

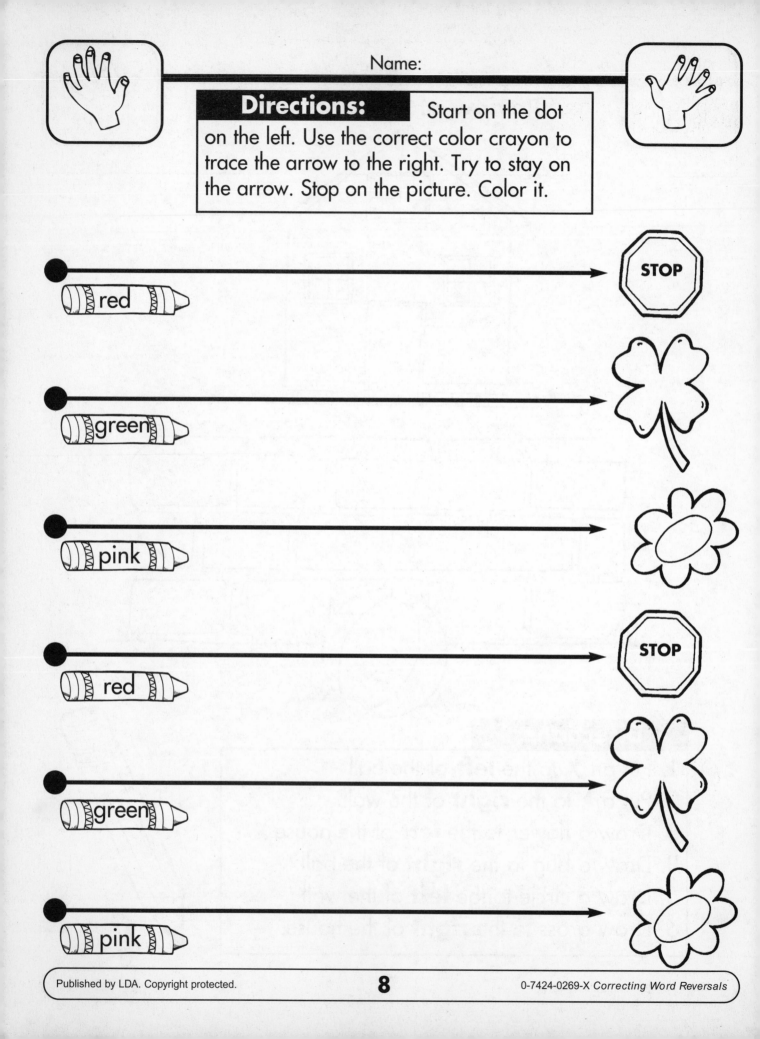

red

green

pink

red

green

pink

STOP

STOP

Name:

Directions: Trace the dotted lines from left to right. Then copy the letters in the correct order on the solid line.

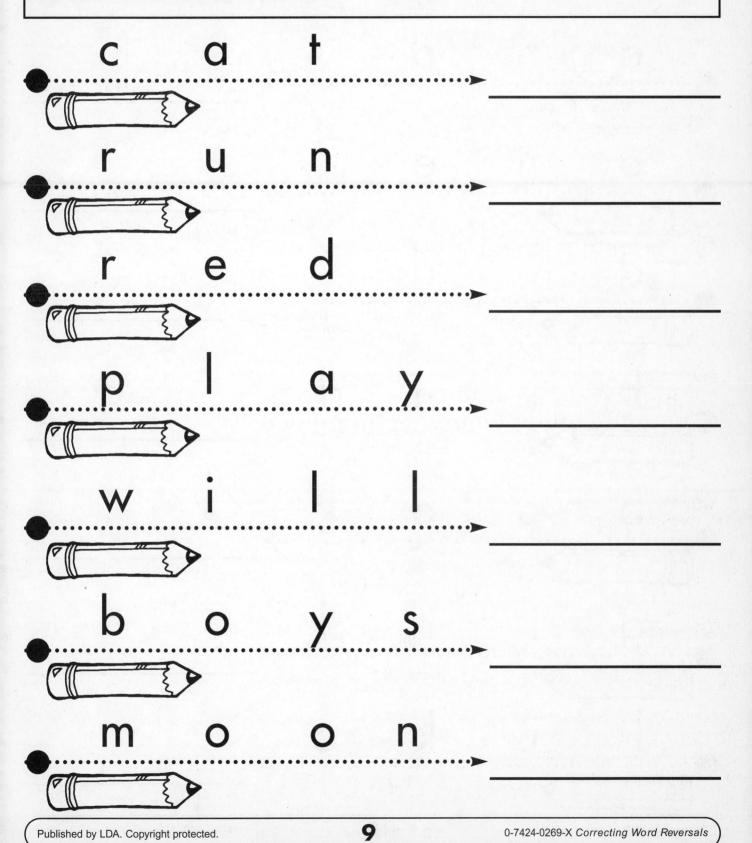

c a t

r u n

r e d

p l a y

w i l l

b o y s

m o o n

0-7424-0269-X *Correcting Word Reversals*

Name: _____

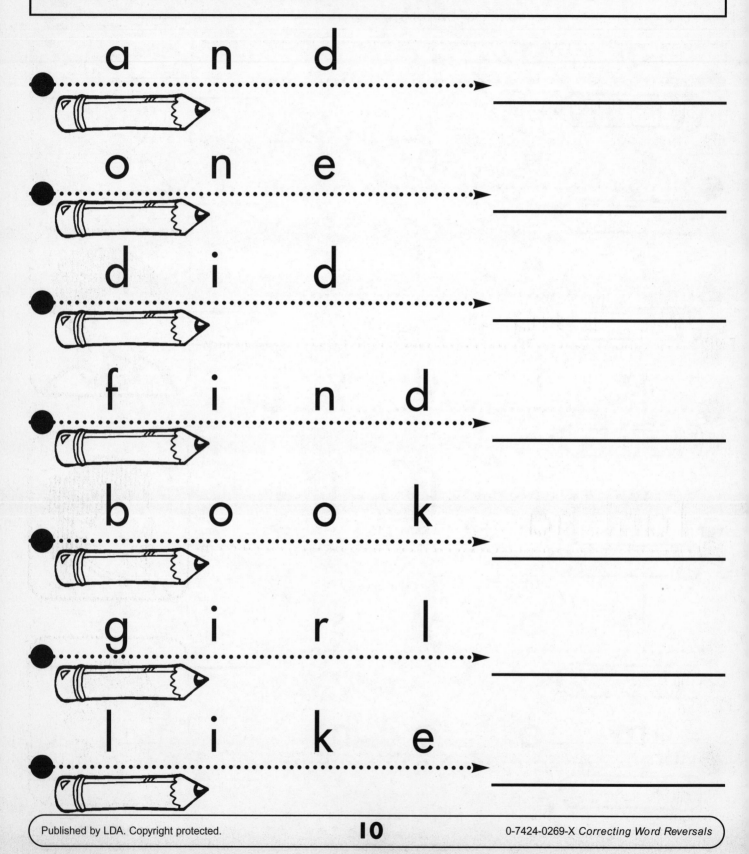

a   n   d

o   n   e

d   i   d

f   i   n   d

b   o   o   k

g   i   r   l

l   i   k   e

Name: _____

Jimmy

●┄┄┄┄┄┄┄┄┄┄┄┄┄┄┄┄┄┄┄┄┄➤

Ms. Ling

●┄┄┄┄┄┄┄┄┄┄┄┄┄┄┄┄┄┄┄┄┄➤

Tanisha

●┄┄┄┄┄┄┄┄┄┄┄┄┄┄┄┄┄┄┄┄┄➤

Juan

●┄┄┄┄┄┄┄┄┄┄┄┄┄┄┄┄┄┄┄┄┄➤

Name: _____

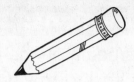

Directions: When writing numbers, you always begin on the left and move toward the right. Trace across the arrow with a pencil. Write the numbers in the box.

3   6   8

1   0   4

8   5   9   7

3   6   1   2

0-7424-0269-X *Correcting Word Reversals*

Name:

Directions: When reading words, you always begin on the left and move toward the right. Trace across each arrow as you read the sentence. Color the picture.

I see the cat.

Look at the tree.

The ball is big.

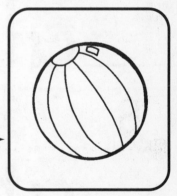

My dog is funny.

Name: _____

Directions:

Trace the beginning of each **b** and complete the letter.
Draw a line from each word to the picture that goes with that word.

bug

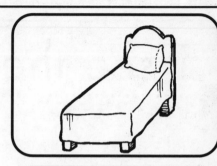

bed

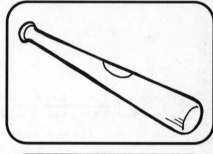

ball

bat

book

14

0-7424-0269-X *Correcting Word Reversals*

Directions:

Trace the beginning of each **b** and complete the letter.
Draw a line from each word to the picture that goes with that word.

ca_l_

bi_l_

tu_l_

Bo_l_

cu_l_

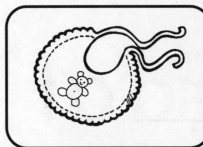

 0-7424-0269-X *Correcting Word Reversals*

Directions:
Trace the beginning of each **b** and complete the letter.
Draw a line from each word to the picture that goes with that word.

__anana

__arn

__utterfly

ra__ __it

__ox

0-7424-0269-X *Correcting Word Reversals*

Directions:

Trace the beginning of each **d** and complete the letter.
Draw a line from each word to the picture that goes with that word.

ro o___

ad o___

la o___

pa o___

sa o___

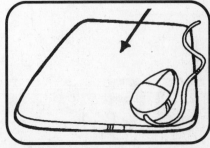

Directions:

Trace the beginning of each **d** and complete the letter.
Draw a line from each word to the picture that goes with that word.

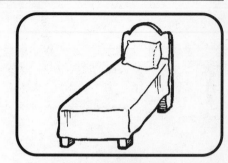

mu o___

da o___

Te o___

li o___

be o___

18

0-7424-0269-X *Correcting Word Reversals*

	g	Name:

Trace the beginning of each **g** and complete the letter.
Draw a line from each word to the picture that goes with that word.

___oldfish

___irl

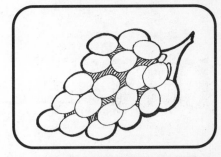

___rapes

___ift

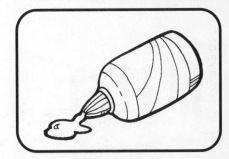

___lue

19

0-7424-0269-X Correcting Word Reversals

Directions:

Trace the beginning of each **p** and complete the letter.
Draw a line from each word to the picture that goes with that word.

ca p

ma p

shi p

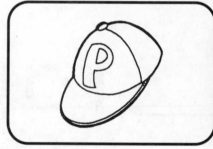

jum p

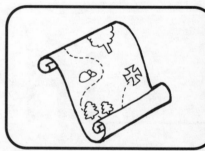

ho p

20

0-7424-0269-X *Correcting Word Reversals*

	Name:
q	

__ueen
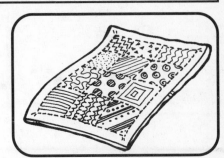

__uilt

__uarter

__uiet

__uartet

21 0-7424-0269-X *Correcting Word Reversals*

Directions:

Trace the beginning of each **s** and complete the letter.
Draw a line from each word to the picture that goes with that word.

___ock

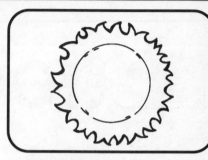

___ad

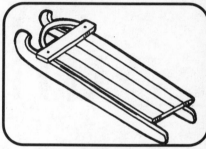

___led

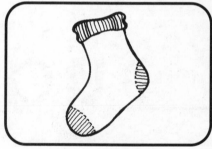

___kate

___un

0-7424-0269-X *Correcting Word Reversals*

Directions:

Trace the beginning of each **s** and complete the letter.
Draw a line from each word to the picture that goes with that word.

hat_s_

cat_s_

dog_s_

log_s_

bee_s_

Directions:

Trace the beginning of each **m** and complete the letter.
Draw a line from each word to the picture that goes with that word.

_m ilk

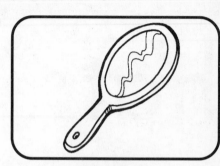

_m ap

_m irror

_m usic

_m an

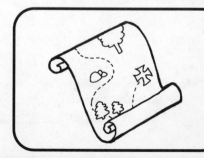

Directions:

Trace the beginning of each **w** and complete the letter.
Draw a line from each word to the picture that goes with that word.

__hale

__heel

__indow

__ater

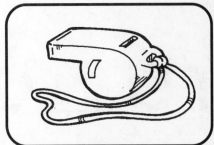

__histle

25

0-7424-0269-X Correcting Word Reversals

Directions:

Trace the beginning of each **z** and complete the letter.
Draw a line from each word to the picture that goes with that word.

di_z_z_y

la_z_y

ma_z_e

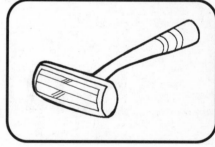

ra_z_or

snee_z_e

0-7424-0269-X *Correcting Word Reversals*

Name: _____

z

Trace the beginning of each **z** and complete the letter.
Draw a line from each word to the picture that goes with that word.

zoo

zebra

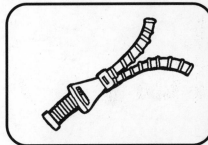

zipper

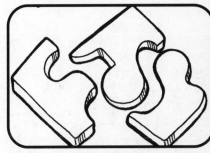

zigzag

puzzle

Directions:

When reading words, touch the first letter of the word and read across from left to right.

was

saw

"Saw" begins with letter "s."
It's followed by an "a."
Add a "w" to this.
You've made a "saw." Hurray!

Directions: Look below and circle all **was** words.

saw	was	asw	saw	aws	was	saw
swa	was	saw	was	was	saw	aws
was	swa	saw	wsa	asw	swa	was
saw	was	saw	was	saw	was	aws
was	asw	saw	was	saw	was	was

How many **was** words did you find? Circle your answer.

  14   **15**   **12**

saw	was	asw	saw	aws	was	saw
swa	was	saw	was	was	saw	aws
wsa	swa	saw	wsa	asw	swa	was
saw	was	saw	was	saw	was	aws
was	asw	saw	was	saw	was	was

How many **was** words did you find? Circle your answer.

11   **13**   **14**

Directions: Look below and circle all **saw** words.

was	swa	was	saw	aws	was	saw
swa	was	saw	was	was	saw	aws
was	swa	saw	wsa	asw	saw	asw
saw	was	saw	was	saw	asw	aws
was	saw	wsa	was	saw	was	was

How many **saw** words did you find? Circle your answer.

10   **9**   **11**

saw	was	saw	asw	saw	was	saw
swa	saw	swa	was	was	saw	swa
saw	asw	aws	swa	saw	was	was
saw	asw	was	swa	was	asw	saw
was	saw	swa	was	saw	swa	was

How many **saw** words did you find? Circle your answer.

12   **11**   **15**

30   0-7424-0269-X *Correcting Word Reversals*

was or saw

Name:

Directions:

Use your yellow crayon to color each space which has **saw** printed in it.
Use your blue crayon to color all spaces which have the word **was.**
When you are finished, answer the riddle.

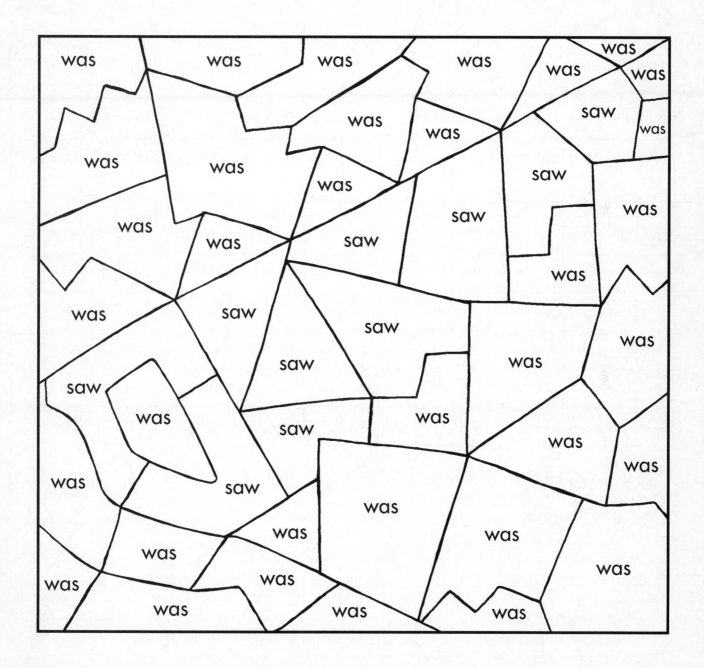

What has teeth but cannot bite? _____

0-7424-0269-X *Correcting Word Reversals*

was or saw

Name:

Directions:

Help Leo the Logger find his missing tool. Follow and color each block that says **saw.** Show Leo the way.

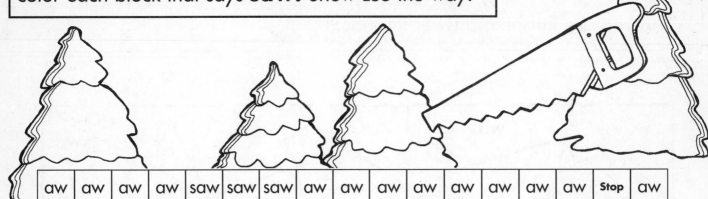

aw	aw	aw	aw	saw	saw	saw	aw	aw	aw	aw	aw	aw	aw	aw	**Stop**	aw
aw	aw	aw	aw	saw	aw	saw	aw	saw	saw	saw	aw	aw	aw	aw	saw	aw
aw	aw	aw	aw	saw	aw	saw	aw	saw	aw	saw	aw	aw	saw	saw	saw	aw
aw	aw	aw	aw	saw	aw	saw	aw	saw	aw	saw	aw	aw	saw	aw	aw	aw
aw	aw	aw	aw	saw	aw	saw	aw	saw	aw	saw	aw	saw	saw	aw	aw	aw
aw	aw	aw	aw	saw	aw	saw	aw	saw	aw	saw	aw	saw	aw	aw	aw	aw
aw	aw	aw	aw	saw	aw	saw	saw	saw	aw	aw	aw	saw	aw	aw	aw	aw
saw	saw	saw	aw	saw	aw	aw	aw	aw	aw	saw	aw	saw	aw	aw	aw	aw
Start ★	aw	saw	saw	saw	aw	aw	aw	aw	aw	saw	saw	saw	aw	aw	aw	aw

Directions:

When reading words, touch the first letter of the word and read across from left to right.

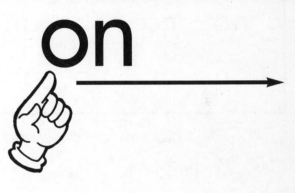

Watch my lips when I say "on."
They form the letter "o."
First, print "o" and then print "n,"
And you are set to go.

Name: _____

Directions:

Look below and circle all **on** words.

no	on	no	no	on	on	no	on	no
no	no	on	on	no	no	on	no	on
no	on	on	on	no	on	no	on	no
no	no	on	on	on	no	on	no	no
on	on	no	on	no	no	on	no	on

How many **on** words did you find? Circle your answer.

  **20**   **18**   **22**

on	no	on	on	no	on	on	no	no
on	no	on	no	no	on	no	on	no
on	no	on	on	no	no	no	on	no
no	on	on	no	no	on	no	on	on
no	no	on	on	no	on	no	on	no

How many **on** words did you find? Circle your answer.

21   **17**   **22**

on or no

Name:

on	on	no	on	on	on	no	on	no
on	no	on	on	no	no	on	no	on
no	on	no	on	no	on	no	on	no
no	no	on	on	on	no	on	no	no
on	on	no	on	no	no	on	no	on

How many **no** words did you find? Circle your answer.

  20   **18**   **21**

no	no	on	no	no	on	on	no	no
no	no	on	no	no	on	no	on	no
on	no	on	on	no	on	no	on	no
no	on	on	no	no	on	no	on	on
no	no	on	on	no	on	no	on	no

How many **no** words did you find? Circle your answer.

22   **24**   **25**

Name:

Directions:

Write **on** or **no** in the blank to complete each sentence. Draw a line to match the correct picture with the sentence.

1. Do not step ____ the flowers.

2. There are ____ cookies in the jar.

3. I look great when I put ____ my hat.

4. I have ____ time to sit and wait.

Directions:

Write **on** or **no** in the blank to complete each sentence. Draw a line to match the correct picture with the sentence.

1. There was ___ one ___ the swing.

2. We had ___ way to get the ball that was ___ top of the house.

3. If the alarm is ___, we will wake up!

4. ___ our trip home, we saw ___ clouds in the sky.

Directions:

When reading words, touch the first letter of the word and read across from left to right.

dad

bad

Dad loves baseball,
so watch his trick.
The ball goes first
and then the stick.

dad or bad

Name:

Directions: Look below and circle all **bad** words.

dad	bad	dab	dab	dad	bad	dad
bad	bad	dad	bab	dab	dab	dad
bad	dad	dad	dab	dad	bad	bad
dad	bad	bab	dab	bad	dad	bad
bab	dad	bad	dab	bad	dab	bab

  How many **bad** words did you find? Circle your answer.

10 **12** **11**

bad	dad	bab	dab	dab	bad	bad
bad	dab	bad	bab	dab	bad	dad
bab	dab	bad	dab	bab	bad	dab
bad	dab	dad	bad	dab	bad	dad
bad	dad	dab	bad	dad	dab	bad

How many **bad** words did you find? Circle your answer.

15 **14** **12**

 0-7424-0269-X *Correcting Word Reversals*

dad or bad

Name:

dab	bad	dad	dab	dad	bad	dad
bad	bad	dad	bab	dad	dab	dad
bad	dad	dad	dab	dad	bad	bad
dad	bad	bab	dad	bad	dad	bad
bab	dad	bad	dad	bad	dad	bab

  How many **dad** words did you find? Circle your answer.

15   **12**   **16**

bad	dad	bab	dad	dab	bad	dad
dad	dab	dad	bab	dad	bad	dad
bab	dad	bad	dad	bab	bad	dad
bad	dab	dad	dad	dab	bad	dad
bad	dad	dad	bad	dad	dab	bad

How many **dad** words did you find? Circle your answer.

16   **15**   **17**

Directions:

Help the animals find Dad's bad hat. Color each block that says **dad**.

dab	bad	bad	bad	bad	bad	bad	bad	bad	bad	bad	bad
bab	bad	bad	dad	dad	dad	dad	dad	dad	bad	bad	bab
dab	bad	bad	dad	bad	bad	bad	bad	dad	bad	bad	bab
bad	bad	bad	dad	bad	bad	bad	bad	dad	bad	bad	bad
bab	dad	dad	███	███	███	███	███	███	dad	dad	dab
bad	dad	bad	bad	bad	bad	bad	bad	bad	bad	dad	dab
dab	dad	dad	dad	dad	dad	dad	dad	dad	dad	dad	bad
bad	bad	bad	bad	bad	bad	bad	bad	bad	bad	bad	dab

Directions:

Read each box. Draw a line from the box to the correct word.

He is ___ the grass.

no

She ___ sleeping.

Me

___? You called me?

was

I have ___ gum.

We

___ are sick.

on

saw

Review

Name: _____

Directions:
Read each box. Draw a line from the box to the correct word.

This is my ____.

bad

I need a ____ of paint.

dad

I am never ____.

dab

I see a ____ bug.

quit

The ____ is happy.

big

pig

Name:

Directions:
Find and circle each incorrect word in the sentences below. Write the correct word on the line.

Oh, no! There is one mistake in each sentence below.

1. I put my hat no.

_____

- - - - - - - - - - - - - -

_____

2. "On, I can't go!"

_____

- - - - - - - - - - - - - -

_____

3. "Turn the light no."

_____

- - - - - - - - - - - - - -

_____

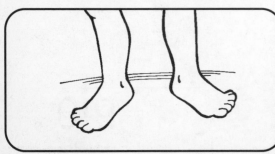

4. I have on shoes on.

_____

- - - - - - - - - - - - - -

_____

Review

Directions:

Find and circle each incorrect word in the sentences below. Write the correct word on the line.

Oh, no! There is one mistake in each sentence below.

1. I have a good bad.

_____

2. She was never dad.

_____

3. Bad has a new hat.

_____

4. I have a dad cold.

_____

Name:

Directions:

Find and circle each incorrect word in the sentences below. Write the correct words on the lines.

Oh, no! There are two mistakes in each sentence below.

1. Pat qut her cat on the quilt.

2. Jim's qal has a puarter.

3. Tim puit qlaying baseball.

4. She will be pueen in the qlay.

Directions:

Find and circle each incorrect word in the sentences below. Write the correct words on the lines.

Oh, no! There are two mistakes in each sentence below.

1. Bob drew a dig picture of his bad.

_____

- - - - - - - - - - - - - - - -

_____

2. The bog has a big dall.

_____

- - - - - - - - - - - - - - - -

_____

3. The doy likes to big.

_____

- - - - - - - - - - - - - - - -

_____

4. She likes to play with her dat and dall.

_____

- - - - - - - - - - - - - - - -

_____

Page 29
Top—14
Bottom—13

Page 30
Top—11
Bottom—12

Page 31

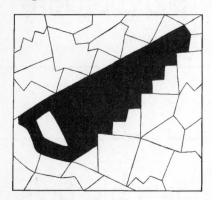

Page 32

aw	aw	aw	aw	saw	saw	aw	aw	aw	aw	aw	aw	aw	Stop	aw
aw	aw	aw	aw	saw	aw	saw	aw	saw	aw	aw	aw	aw	saw	aw
aw	aw	aw	saw	aw	aw	aw	aw	saw	aw	saw	aw	aw	aw	aw
aw	aw	aw	saw	aw	saw	aw	aw	saw	aw	aw	saw	aw	aw	aw
aw	aw	aw	saw	aw	saw	aw	aw	saw	aw	saw	aw	aw	aw	aw
aw	aw	aw	saw	aw	saw	aw	aw	saw	aw	saw	aw	aw	aw	aw
aw	aw	aw	aw	saw	aw	aw	aw	aw	aw	saw	aw	aw	aw	aw
saw	saw	aw	saw	aw	aw	aw	aw	aw	aw	saw	saw	aw	aw	aw
Start	aw	saw	saw	saw	aw	aw	aw	aw	aw	saw	saw	aw	aw	aw

Page 34
Top—22
Bottom—22

Page 35
Top—21
Bottom—25

Page 36
1. on
2. no
3. on
4. no

Page 37
1. no, on
2. no, on
3. on
4. On, no

Page 39
Top—12
Bottom—14

Page 40
Top—15
Bottom—16

Page 41

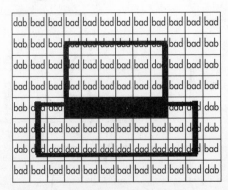

Page 42
He is <u>on</u> the grass.
She <u>was</u> sleeping.
<u>Me</u>? You called me.
I have <u>no</u> gum.
<u>We</u> are sick.

Page 43
This is my <u>dad</u>.
I need a <u>dab</u> of paint.
I am never <u>bad</u>.
I see a <u>big</u> bug.
The <u>pig</u> is happy.

Page 44
I put my hat <u>on</u>.
"<u>No</u>, I can't go!"
Turn the light <u>on</u>."
I have <u>no</u> shoes on.

Page 45
I have a good <u>dad</u>.
She was never <u>bad</u>.
<u>Dad</u> has a new hat.
I have a <u>bad</u> cold.

Page 46
Pat <u>put</u> her cat on
the <u>quilt</u>.
Jim's <u>pal</u> has a <u>quarter</u>.
Tim <u>quit</u> <u>playing</u> baseball.
She will be <u>queen</u> in the <u>play</u>.

Page 47
Bob drew a <u>big</u> picture of his
<u>dad</u>.
The <u>dog</u> has a big <u>ball</u>.
The <u>boy</u> likes to <u>dig</u>.
She likes to play with her <u>bat</u>
and <u>ball</u>.